JOURNEY THROUGH
RUSSIA

ANITA GANERI

W
FRANKLIN WATTS
LONDON•SYDNEY

Franklin Watts
Published in Great Britain in 2018 by The Watts Publishing Group

Credits
Series Editor: Amy Stephenson
Editor: Elise Short
Series Designer: Emma DeBanks
Picture Researcher: Diana Morris

Picture credits: Igor Akimov/Dreamstime: 27r. aleksandr4300/Shutterstock: 5br. Alex99/Shutterstock: 27tl. Lukas Blazek/Dreamstime: 16b. Larisa Blinova/Shutterstock: 5c. Brother Luck/Alamy: 29t. Caro/Sebastien/Alamy: 11b. Chelovek/Dreamstime: 22. Chelovek/Shutterstock: 23c. Alexander Cher/Shutterstock: 7tcb. 7trb. Dennis Donohue/Dreamstime: 25t. Sergey Eremin/Dreamstime: 15tr. Galina Ermolaevina/Dreamstime:10-11b. Anastaia Fisechko/Shuttertock: 7cr. FotograFFF/Shutterstock: 6c. fyb/Shutterstock: 6tl. Georgiy Golorin/Dreamstime: 17t. Igor Grochev/Shutterstock: 13b. Igor Gushchin/Dreamstime: 28. Images & Stories/Alamy: 20. Irinabal18/Dreamstime: 6bl, 11t. ITAR-TASS/Alamy:18. Evgeny Karandaev/Shutterstock: 7tlb. Kiboka/Dreamstime: 9t. Sergey Kichigin/Dreamstime: 6tr. Alexei Koganov/Dreamstime: 3b. Mikhail Kokhanchiko/Dreamstime: 17b. Oleg Kosov/Dreamstime: 7tl. i Leysen/Shutterstock: 7cl. Vladimir Melnik/Dreamstime: 10cl. Trevor Mogg/Alamy: 7tc,19b. Evengiy Muhortov/Dreamstime: 14. Odua/Dreamstime: 7clb. Olenyok/Shutterstock: 27b. Opsmedia/Dreasmtimes: 29b. Irina Ovchinnikova/Shutterstock: 7tr, 25b. Vlad Ozerov/Shutterstock: 8. Sergey Ponomarev/Dreamstime: 7bc. Valeriya Popova/Shutterstock: 13t. Prostock Studio/Shutterstock: 6cr. Refat/Shutterstock: 6tcb. Reidphoto/Dreamstime: front cover, 12. Marco Rubino/Shutterstock: 9cl. schankz/Shutterstock: 6tc. Ilyn Sergey/Shutterstock: 19t. Elena Shchipkova/Dreamstime: 21t. Shinobi/Shutterstock: 15b. Natalia Sidarova/Shutterstock: 15tl. Sputnik/Alamy: 24, 26. Mircea Predat Struteanu/Dreamstime: 1. s-ts/Shutterstock: 6cl. Sunflower/Shutterstock: 4t. Peter SVET Photo/Shutterstock: 9cr. Pavel Trofimov/Shutterstock:21tr. Valery2007/Dreamstime: 7br. Dmitry Vereshchagin/Shutterstock: 7crb. vicspacewalker/Shutterstock: 13c. With God/Shutterstock: 23b. Bukhta Yurii/Shutterstock: 7cb. Serg Zastavkin/Shutterstock: 4-5b. Zelennskaya/Shutterstock: 6tlb.

ISBN: 978 1 4451 5621 7

Printed in China

Franklin Watts
An imprint of
Hachette Children's Group
Part of The Watts Publishing Group
Carmelite House
50 Victoria Embankment
London EC4Y 0DZ

An Hachette UK Company
www.hachette.co.uk

www.franklinwatts.co.uk

CONTENTS

WELCOME TO RUSSIA!

Добро пожаловать в Россию! (Dobro pozhalovat v Rossiyu!) Welcome to Russia! Covering an area of 17,075,200 sq km, the Russian Federation is the largest country in the world. It reaches from Europe in the west to Asia in the east, and from the Arctic in the north to the Caucasus in the south. It would take years to explore the entire country, but your trip around Russia will transport you from one side to the other with some amazing sights and experiences along the way!

▲ The Russian flag has three equal stripes in white, blue and red.

Russia facts

Russia has a population of 144 million people. It is so big that, from Kalingrad in the west to the Kamchatka Peninsula in the east, it covers 11 time zones. When people are going to bed at 11 p.m. in the capital, Moscow, others are already getting up at 8 a.m. to start the next day in Kamchatka. Russia shares land borders with 14 countries (see map on pages 6–7). Some of these countries, along with Russia, were once part of the Union of Soviet Socialist Republics (USSR), a communist state that existed from 1922 until its overthrow in 1991. The USSR was often known as the Soviet Union.

▼ The Altai Mountains tower over the grasslands of the Eurasian steppe.

Story of Russia

The story of Russia begins with a people called the Slavs who spread across Europe from c. 200-700 CE. The medieval state of Rus developed in the 800s, and it took Orthodox Christianity as its state religion. From the 1400s, Russia was ruled by tsars (emperors), and by the 1700s, the Russian Empire extended far and wide. The reign of the tsars ended in 1917, with the February Revolution and the eventual creation of the world's first communist state, the USSR.

Seeing and tasting Russia

Your trip will take you to some of the places that make up Russia's wide range of landscapes, such as the Ural Mountains, the Caucasus and Kamchatka. There are vast grasslands, stretches of thick forest and icy tundra along the Arctic coast. There are also beautiful lakes. You will get to see many of these landscapes as you take various modes of transportation, including a very special train – right across Russia. On the way you will be able to try some Russian specialities, including *borsch* (beetroot soup, see above), *blinis* (small pancakes) and *kulebiaka* (fish pie).

Russian language

Russian is a Slavic language, and it uses the Cyrillic alphabet. It is the official language in Russia, although many other languages are also spoken across the country. Here are a few useful phrases to help you on your journey:

Zdravstvuyte – hello

Da svidaniya – goodbye

Pozhaluysta – please

Spasiba – thank you

Da – yes

Nyet – no

Kak dela? – how are you?

► Street signs in Russia are written in the Cyrillic alphabet.

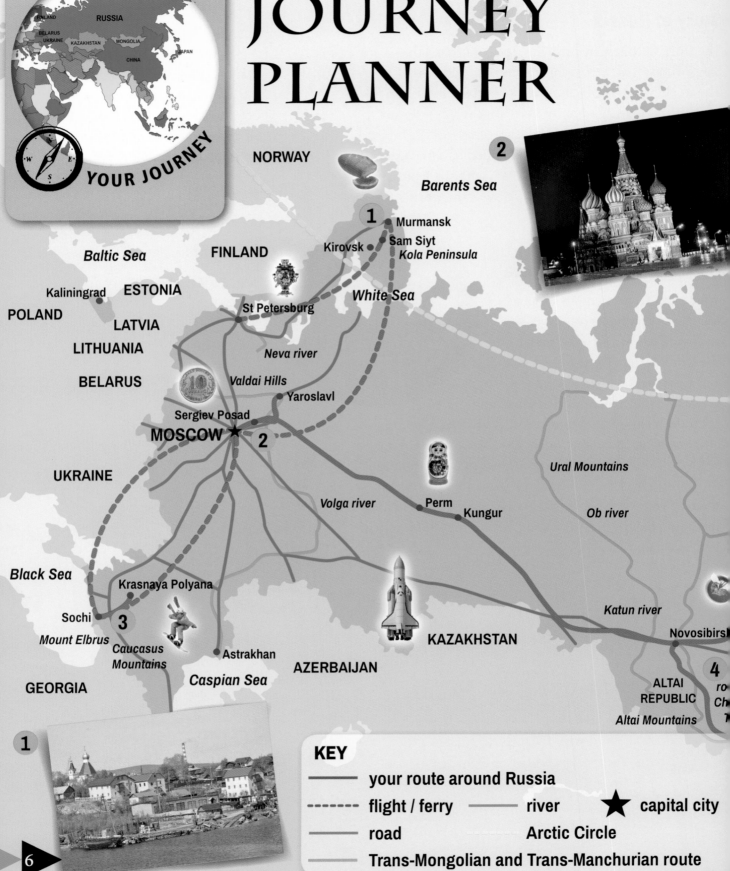

JOURNEY PLANNER

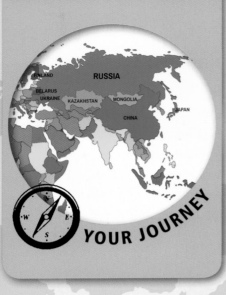

YOUR JOURNEY

NORWAY

Barents Sea

2

1 Murmansk

Kirovsk Sam Siyt
Kola Peninsula

Baltic Sea FINLAND

White Sea

Kaliningrad ESTONIA

POLAND

LATVIA

St Petersburg

LITHUANIA

Neva river

BELARUS

Valdai Hills

Yaroslavl

Sergiev Posad

MOSCOW ★ **2**

UKRAINE

Ural Mountains

Volga river Perm

Ob river

Kungur

Black Sea

Krasnaya Polyana

Katun river

Sochi

3

Novosibirsk

Mount Elbrus *Caucasus Mountains* Astrakhan

KAZAKHSTAN

AZERBAIJAN

4

GEORGIA *Caspian Sea*

ALTAI
REPUBLIC

Altai Mountains

1

KEY

——— your route around Russia

------- flight / ferry ——— river ★ capital city

——— road Arctic Circle

——— Trans-Mongolian and Trans-Manchurian route

6

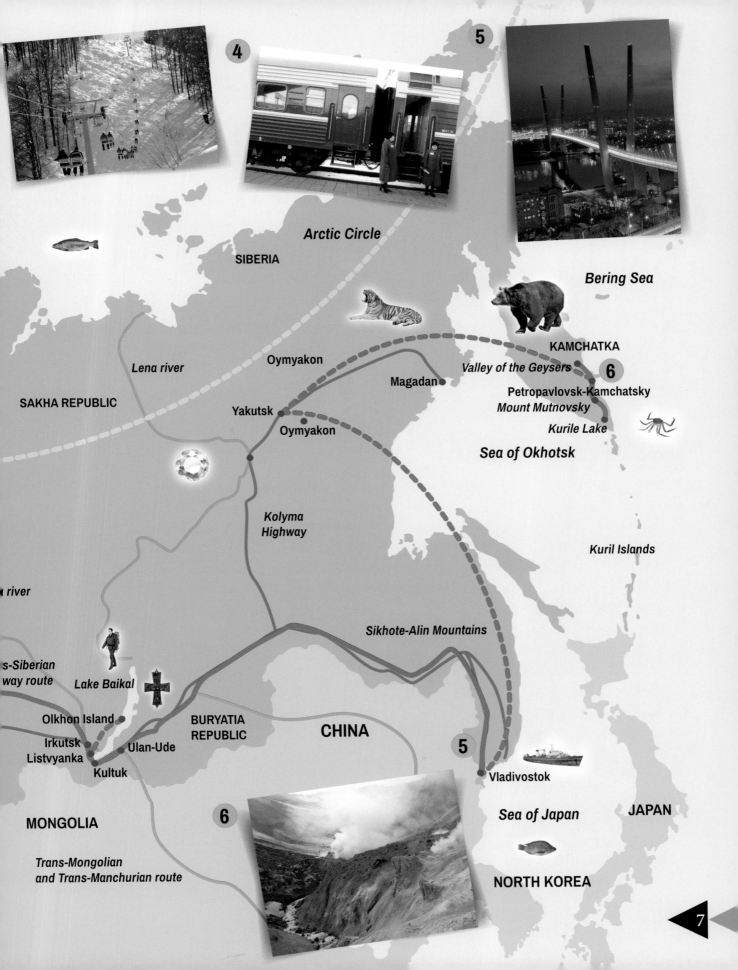

4

5

Arctic Circle

SIBERIA

Bering Sea

Lena river

Oymyakon

Magadan

KAMCHATKA

Valley of the Geysers

6

SAKHA REPUBLIC

Yakutsk

Petropavlovsk-Kamchatsky
Mount Mutnovsky

Oymyakon

Kurile Lake

Sea of Okhotsk

*Kolyma
Highway*

Kuril Islands

river

Sikhote-Alin Mountains

*s-Siberian
way route*

Lake Baikal

Olkhon Island

**BURYATIA
REPUBLIC**

CHINA

5

Irkutsk

Ulan-Ude

Listvyanka

Kultuk

Vladivostok

6

Sea of Japan

JAPAN

MONGOLIA

*Trans-Mongolian
and Trans-Manchurian route*

NORTH KOREA

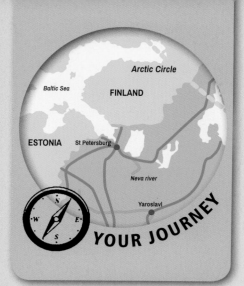

YOUR JOURNEY

ARRIVING IN ST PETERSBURG

You arrive by cruise ship to start your Russian journey in St Petersburg, in the northwest of the country. This famous and historic city is built on the delta of the Neva river, as it flows out into the Baltic Sea. Home to around 5 million people, the city sits on the many islands that make up the delta. Criss-crossed with canals, it is sometimes known as the 'Venice of the North'.

Introducing St Petersburg

St Petersburg is an important port, as well as a financial and industrial centre. There are shipbuilding yards and huge cargo ships on both banks of the Neva river. The city was founded by Tsar Peter I (Peter the Great) in 1703. Peter brought in thousands of peasants and prisoners-of-war to build his grand new city – and many died in the terrible working and weather conditions. In 1712, Peter made St Petersburg the capital of his Russian empire. You start your tour where the city was founded – at the Peter and Paul Fortress on Zayachy Island. In the middle of the fortress is the Cathedral of Saints Peter and Paul, with its spectacular golden spire reaching 122 m into the sky. Climb the cathedral's bell tower to experience the views across this spectacular city.

▶ St Petersburg Plaza on the Neva river is the home of the St Petersburg Bank, the tallest building.

A centre of culture and economy

From Zayachy Island, you can cross the Neva river by one of St Petersburg's 342 bridges or take a boat ride along the magnificent waterfront. From here, walk to the Hermitage Museum, part of which is housed in the lavish Winter Palace. This huge museum contains more than three million works of art. It is said that it would take 11 years to view everything in the collection! It is one of many historic places that attract millions of tourists to the city each year. Tourism is big business in St Petersburg and a vital part of the city's economy.

▼ The Winter Palace was built for Tsarina (Empress) Catherine the Great in 1754–62.

▲ The Church of the Saviour on Spilled Blood.

Dome dazzler

You walk along one of the city's many canals to your final stop – the Church of the Saviour on Spilled Blood. Its name comes from its history; it was built on the spot where Tsar Alexander II was assassinated in 1881. Inside, every inch of its walls is decorated with colourful mosaics, and its roof is topped by five dazzling, onion-shaped domes.

▲ White Nights festival

White Nights Festival

From mid-June until the beginning of July, it is light all day and all night in St Petersburg. These 'White Nights' happen because the city lies so far north that the Sun never dips down below the horizon in midsummer. In St Petersburg, people make the most of these magical nights with festivals, concerts and performances of opera and ballet at the beautiful Mariinsky Theatre. Over one million people turn out to line the banks of the Neva river and watch the Scarlet Sails. This is an open-air event with spectacular fireworks that ends with the appearance of a beautiful sailing ship with scarlet sails on the river.

9

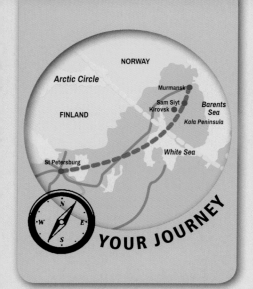

INTO THE ARCTIC

Your flight from St Petersburg's Pulkovo Airport takes you 1,330 km north to the city of Murmansk, on the shores of the Barents Sea. Murmansk lies just inside the Arctic Circle. The average winter temperature is around -10°C, but it can sometimes drop as low as -39°C. For 40 days in December and January, the people of Murmansk live in constant darkness. The city is so far north that the Sun never rises above the horizon. This time of darkness is called the 'polar night'.

▲ This is one of the largest, most powerful nuclear-powered icebreakers in the world. *50 Years of Victory* can break through ice up to 2.5 m thick.

Warm waters

Murmansk is an important port and one of the largest in Russia. Despite its northern location, the warming waters of the North Atlantic Drift usually keep the port free of ice all year round. The North Atlantic Drift is an ocean current that starts far away in the Gulf of Mexico, where it is known as the Gulf Stream. Murmansk's port is home to large numbers of commercial fishing boats, and to Russia's fleet of nuclear-powered icebreakers. These ships are specially designed to smash their way through the thick sea ice further north. From here, you can take a cruise on a nuclear icebreaker all the way to the North Pole.

The Kola Peninsula

To the east of Murmansk lies the Kola Peninsula – 100,000 sq km of land that separates the Barents Sea and the White Sea. This is a huge area of tundra, lakes, birch forests and towering mountains where it is possible to go skiing. To explore, you travel to Kirovsk on a shared minibus-taxi, called a *marshrutka*. Kirovsk is a mining town. The Kola Peninsula has the world's biggest deposits of a mineral called apatite, used to make fertilisers, which help plants grow. If you arrive in winter, stay and watch a local tradition – taking a dip in a frozen lake by cutting a hole in the ice and jumping in!

▲ Colourful houses line some parts of the Kola Peninsula.

▼ On a polar night, this road through the icy Kola Peninsula doesn't get any darker.

The Sami people

The Sami people were the original inhabitants of the Kola Peninsula. Traditionally, they lived by fishing, and herding sheep and reindeer. You end your visit to the Kola Peninsula at Sam-Siyt, a Sami village, where you eat a traditional Sami meal of reindeer sausage and *vyar* (reindeer meat soup).

▶ There are only 2,000 Sami people living in Russia.

Exploiting the Arctic

It is likely that there are massive reserves of oil and gas in the Russian Arctic. Russia is the world's largest exporter of both, so these reserves are very important for the Russian economy. Many people believe that oil and gas exploration is a threat to the delicate ecosystems of the Arctic. But Russia also has more than 100 official nature reserves – areas where wildlife and ecosystems are protected. The biggest is the Great Arctic State Nature Reserve, which covers many thousands of kilometres in Russia's northernmost regions.

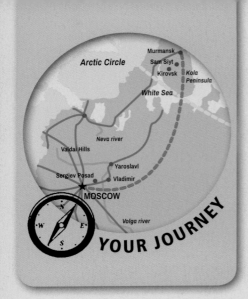

YOUR JOURNEY

MURMANSK TO MOSCOW

Another marshrutka takes you back to Murmansk Airport, where you board a flight south to Moscow, the capital of Russia. Home to 12.2 million people, Moscow is more than 800 years old, and grew up around a wooden hilltop fortress, or *kremlin*. Today, the Kremlin in Moscow is the centre of government and the home of the Russian president. You start your tour of Moscow outside the impressive Kremlin walls, by Lenin's Mausoleum in Red Square.

Vladimir Lenin

Famous communist figure, Vladimir Lenin, was one of the leaders of the Russian Revolution in 1917. When Lenin died in 1924, his body was preserved for future generations to see. More than 90 years later you can still go to see the embalmed body of Lenin lying on a huge bed in his mausoleum.

▶ The onion domes of St Basil's Cathedral are a dramatic feature of Red Square.

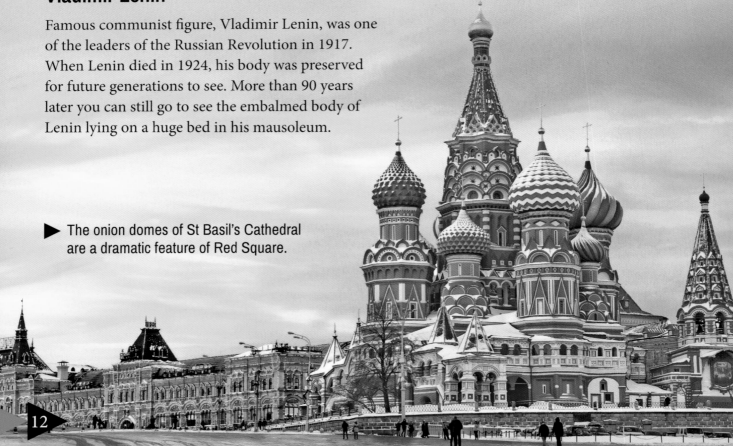

Moscow's amazing metro

One of the easiest and cheapest ways to travel round Moscow is by metro. You will realise that this is no ordinary subway system. The Moscow Metro was built in the 1930s, when the USSR was under the control of the dictator, Joseph Stalin. He ordered the builders to create something spectacular beneath the Moscow streets – 'palaces for the people'. It has exquisite chandeliers, statues, and hallways decorated with paintings and mosaics, many of which tell a story from Russia's communist past. Today, the Moscow Metro is the busiest in Europe with over 330 km of track, carrying more than 2.4 billion passengers every year.

▲ Travelling on the Moscow Metro is like taking a trip through an art gallery.

► US astronaut J. Williams photographed during spacewalk training in water in Star City.

Star City

About 25 km outside Moscow, Star City was once a top-secret location closed to outsiders. Since Russian cosmonaut Yuri Gagarin became the first human to go into space in 1961, this is where cosmonauts and some astronauts train for missions into space. Today, Star City is open to visitors. You can practise controlling a spacecraft as it blasts off into space, try on a spacesuit, cook and eat space food, and find out what it is like to experience zero gravity on the IL-76 MDK laboratory aircraft.

Must-see destinations in Moscow

The Kremlin – for 800 years of Russian history

St Basil's Cathedral on Red Square – built by Ivan the Terrible

Armoury Chamber – look out for the Fabergé eggs

GUM – a spectacular and elegant department store

Bolshoi Theatre – home of the world-famous Bolshoi Ballet

► This is one of sixty-nine jewelled eggs created by Peter Carl Fabergé.

13

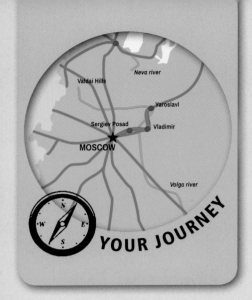

YOUR JOURNEY

THE GOLDEN RING

If you need a break from the hustle and bustle of Moscow, you could travel by bus into the countryside beyond the city – a land of dense woods and forests, dotted with villages of wooden houses. The cities and towns to the northeast of Moscow are often known as the 'Golden Ring'. They are some of the oldest in Russia, containing many important places linked to the Russian Orthodox Church.

Dachas

You will not be the only person heading out of the city! Summers in Moscow can be very hot (up to 30°C) and many people who live and work there try to escape the city at weekends and during holidays to go to their country houses – or *dachas*. People love to grow fruit and vegetables in the gardens of their dachas, and to relax, away from city life. Through the bus window, you'll spot some of these simple houses, painted in bright colours and surrounded by gardens.

▼ There are dachas dotted all over the Russian countryside.

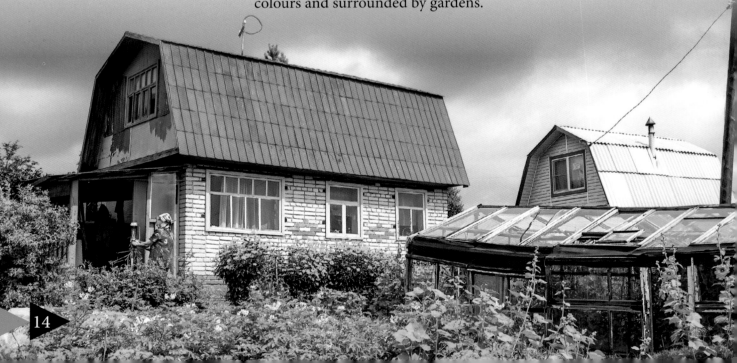

◀ The Trinity Monastery

▶ This Russian Orthodox icon represents Mary and the baby Jesus.

Russia's patron saint

Your bus takes you to one of the Golden Ring towns, Sergiev Posad, where you visit the Trinity Monastery. This monastery is one of the holiest places in all of Russia, and is visited by pilgrims all year round. It was founded by Sergius of Radonezh who, in 1422, became patron saint of Russia. It is a massive complex of buildings, surrounded by high, white walls.

Volga town

Next, a train journey takes you to another Golden Ring town, Yaroslavl, which lies on the mighty Volga river. From the 1600s to the 1900s, Yaroslavl was a thriving river port, and its wealthy merchants paid for many beautiful churches to be built across the whole town. After walking round the historic city centre, take a boat trip down the Volga – the longest river in Europe at 3,530 km. The Volga rises in the Valdai Hills northwest of Moscow, and flows into the Caspian Sea. It drains a vast area of western Russia and along the way provides irrigation for farming, and hydroelectric power from its reservoirs.

Religion in Russia

In Christianity, the Orthodox Church forms one of three main groups (alongside Roman Catholic and Protestant). The Russian Orthodox Church is a separate branch with its own leader, the Patriarch of Moscow and all Russia. It is the main religion in Russia – around 75 per cent of Russians are Orthodox Christians. Other religions include Islam (around 5 per cent of the population), Protestantism and Catholicism, Judaism and Buddhism (around 1 per cent each). Services in Russian Orthodox churches are often candle-lit, and almost all of the words are chanted or sung. Icons are also important – these images of Jesus Christ and the Christian saints are often painted on wood. They are treasured and venerated by worshippers, who consider them to represent God.

▶ The Volga is a vital route for trade, with cargoes such as petroleum, coal, crops, salt, machinery and cars transported by barge.

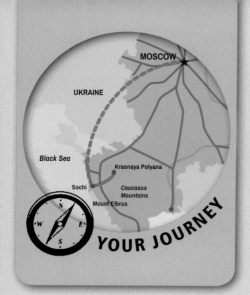

MOSCOW

UKRAINE

Black Sea

Krasnaya Polyana

Sochi

Caucasus
Mountains

Mount Elbrus

MOSCOW TO SOCHI

The next stage of your trip takes you to a part of Russia called the Caucasus, named after the impressive mountain range at the heart of the region. The Caucasus lies between the Black Sea and the Caspian Sea, and it is where the continents of Europe and Asia meet. There are plenty of outdoor activities to choose from, such as horse riding, white-water rafting, skiing and climbing amongst the soaring mountain peaks.

Holiday resort

Your flight from Moscow takes you to Sochi, a resort on the Black Sea coast. In the late 1800s, Sochi became a fashionable holiday destination for wealthy Russians. It became even more popular in the 1930s, when Stalin built a dacha near the city. In 2014, Sochi was the host city for the Winter Olympics – although all the skiing action actually took place at Krasnaya Polyana, about 50 km away, where a massive ski complex was built for the event. Today, a high-speed rail link makes it easy to get from Sochi to the ski slopes in just 75 minutes.

▼ The area around Sochi is popular for winter sports, such as snowboarding.

◀ Mount Elbrus is the tenth tallest peak in the world.

Mount Elbrus

The Caucasus Mountains were formed millions of years ago as the result of a collision between two of the tectonic plates that form the Earth's surface. The highest peak in the Caucasus is also Europe's highest mountain – Mount Elbrus at 5,642 m. Elbrus is a dormant volcano. The last time it erupted was around 2,000 years ago, although there are ongoing signs of volcanic activity. For a breathtaking ride, take a cable car and a very chilly chairlift ride up to 3,800 m. Then you can either ski down, or if you've booked a professional guide, this is where you start the climb to the twin peaks of the mountain's summit.

Georgian treats

South of Sochi, the Caucasus form the country border between Russia and Georgia. Georgia, together with neighbouring Armenia and Azerbaijan, were part of the Soviet Union until 1991. Many restaurants in Russia still serve food from these former Soviet republics. Try out some typical Georgian dishes including: *satsivi* – a creamy walnut sauce, *khinkali* – dumplings stuffed with meat and spices, and *khachapuri* – a cheesy bread topped with an egg.

Mineral treatments

On the northern side of the Caucasus, there is an area where many natural springs emerge from the ground. The minerals in these waters are believed to be good for all sorts of ailments, and people have been coming to this region to treat their illnesses since the 1800s. Russians still visit today to experience the springs and mud treatments, and to relax in the clean mountain air.

▲ Khinkali dumplings

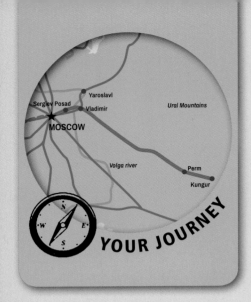

TRANS-SIBERIAN RAILWAY

After your time in the Caucasus, you fly back to Moscow for the start of one of the most famous journeys in the world – the epic trip across Russia on board the Trans-Siberian Railway, built between 1891 and 1905. This classic rail journey transports you from one side of Russia to the other, from Moscow to Vladivostok on the Sea of Japan – a total of 9,258 km. The train journey takes seven days, crossing from Europe into Asia. You'll travel through eight time zones!

Perm-36

Your journey east from Moscow takes you through the dramatic Ural Mountains. These mountains stretch for 2,500 km from the Arctic Ocean southwards across Russia, and mark the divide between Europe to the west and Asia to the east. You make a stop at Perm, an industrial city that was the centre of Soviet weapons manufacturing in the Second World War (1939–45). You visit Perm-36. It is the only gulag preserved in Russia as a reminder of the brutality of the communist regime.

The gulag was a system of forced labour camps in the USSR. People convicted of crimes were sent to these camps, including political prisoners who disagreed with the communist government. Millions of people were sent to gulags, and many died as a result of the appalling conditions and exhausting work. There were gulags all over Russia, but Perm-36 is the only one left standing and it is now a museum.

▲ The Perm-36 gulag

Ice cave

▲ Inside the ice cave, there are spectacular icicles.

A short distance from Perm, at Kungur, you visit a famous cave. You need to dress warmly to head into the cave with your guide. This is a karst cave – formed as water has eaten away at the rock over thousands of years. The temperature inside the cave remains below freezing, even when it is hot outside, and after only a few minutes underground you'll start to feel the chill! Take a guided tour of the cave and its amazing ice formations. The longest tour takes in 2 km of passageways.

Trans-Siberian routes

There are in fact three different Trans-Siberian routes that cross Russia. All three routes follow the same line east out of Moscow to Lake Baikal (see pages 22–23). Here, the routes split – the Trans-Siberian continues east to Vladivostok, the Trans-Mongolian heads south through Mongolia, following an ancient trade route across the Gobi Desert to Beijing, China, while the Trans-Manchurian takes a long loop through China, also terminating in Beijing. As well as carrying passengers, the Trans-Siberian railway is a vital freight route, with cargo trains carrying goods between Europe and Asia.

▼ The train attendants welcome you aboard the longest railway line in the world.

MECT-26

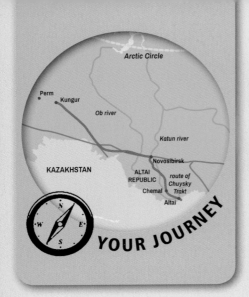

ALTAI REPUBLIC

Back on the train, you head to your next stop of Novosibirsk. This city was founded in 1893 when workers began to build a railway bridge across the Ob river for the Trans-Siberian Railway. Today, the city is the third largest in Russia and an important centre for industry and transport. The railway provides an east-west link, while major roads and the Ob river provide routes from north to south.

Altai people

From Novosibirsk, catch a bus south to the Altai Republic – a region of beautiful lakes and mountains. Although it is called a republic, it is still part of the Russian Federation. This region is the traditional home of the Altai people, who were originally nomads, moving from one place to another with their sheep, goats, horses and cattle. Today, the population of the Altai Republic is made up of around 30 per cent Altai, and 70 per cent Russians, and most Altai live settled lives. Your first stop is Chemal, where you can visit some traditional Altai homes – wooden huts rather like yurts, called *aily*.

▼ An Altai boy looks after the family's yaks.

▼ The Katun river is perfect for white-water rafting.

▲ At 2,000 m high, the water in the Karakol Lakes comes from the nearby glaciers and is very cold.

Outdoor thrills

Near Chemal there are a variety of adventures to choose from in the spectacular landscape of Altai. You can visit a deep gorge where you can go white-water rafting on the Katun river. From here, you can also travel up into the mountains on horseback for a multi-day trek that takes you to the stunning, turquoise blue Karakol Lakes.

Chuysky Trakt

You hire a car and a driver for the next part of your journey on the Chuysky Trakt trail. This road starts in Novosibirsk, and stretches nearly 1,000 km south through Altai to the Russian border with Mongolia. Originally used by traders to take goods by horseback from Asia to Europe, the old mountain track was replaced in the 1930s by an asphalt road, built mainly by gulag prisoners. From the Seminsky Pass, looking southwards, the views are breathtaking!

Siberia: history and climate

East of the Ural Mountains, Siberia makes up about three-quarters of Russia's total territory, but is home to only a quarter of the Russian population. This massive region became part of Russia in the 1600s and 1700s, but it was the construction of the Trans-Siberian Railway that brought people from other parts of Russia to live there. The Ural Mountains form a barrier that prevents the warm winds from the Atlantic Ocean reaching Siberia, so the region has a cool, dry climate. Summers are warm enough to grow fruit, such as watermelons, in the south. Average winter temperatures for the whole region are around -25°C, but these drop lower in the Arctic north.

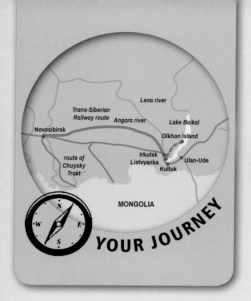

YOUR JOURNEY

LAKE BAIKAL

Back in Novosibirsk, jump back on the Trans-Siberian Railway and continue your journey east. This part of your journey takes a day and a half. Out of the window, you'll see endless forests of birch trees and small villages with wooden houses as you cross eastern Siberia. Your destination is the city of Irkutsk, near the southern end of Lake Baikal.

▼ Nicknamed the 'Pearl of Siberia', Lake Baikal is the world's oldest lake at 25 million years old.

Exploring Lake Baikal

Lake Baikal is the oldest and deepest lake on Earth. Formed around 25 to 30 million years ago, the lake is 636 km long, and up to 1,637 m deep. It contains around 20 per cent of the unfrozen freshwater on our planet. Baikal lies on a rift – where two of Earth's tectonic plates are moving apart. This movement of the Earth's crust is felt in the region as small earthquakes every few years. More than 300 rivers feed this huge lake, but it is drained by just one river, the Angara, at the southern end.

Olkhon Island

To reach the southern end of Lake Baikal, take a ride on a hydrofoil from Irkutsk port on the Angara river to the town of Listvyanka. From here, you can jump on a ferry to Olkhon Island, half way up the western shore of the lake. The different landscapes on the island are surprising – from dramatic mountains reaching 1,276 m high that plunge straight into the sea, to forests and even a small desert.

Touring Lake Baikal

Before setting off on your next adventure, try a Lake Baikal speciality – a white fish called omul, considered a great delicacy. You are now ready to walk part of the Great Baikal Trail. If you don't feel like walking, you can jump on the Circum-Baikal Railway, which runs along the side of the lake to Kultuk.

Lake Baikal in winter

In winter, Lake Baikal freezes. You can skate, cycle and even drive across the thick ice of the frozen lake – although you need to do this with an experienced guide. The lake ice forms incredible shapes and caves, and because the water is so clean the ice is very pure. You can also try your hand at ice fishing through a hole cut in the ice.

▼ The Circum-Baikal Railway was an amazing feat of engineering when it was built 100 years ago, as it has 39 tunnels to take the railway through the mountains that line the shore.

Lake Baikal wildlife

Lake Baikal is home to more than 2,000 different species of animals and plants, many of which are found nowhere else on Earth. The Baikal seal is the world's only freshwater seal. It is estimated that there are up to 100,000 seals living in all parts of the lake. Brown bears, as well as elk, deer and wolves live in the mountains that fringe the lake shores. There are also fish, such as *Golomyanka* (fat fish), and hundreds of species of invertebrates.

► It is something of a mystery how Baikal seals came to live in Lake Baikal. They are estimated to have inhabited Lake Baikal for some two million years.

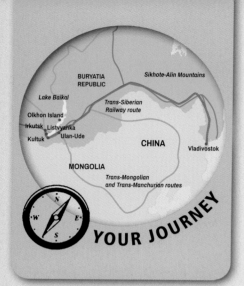

IRKUTSK TO VLADIVOSTOK

The last leg of your Trans-Siberian Railway journey takes you to Ulan-Ude, and from there to Vladivostok in the far east of Russia. In Ulan-Ude, you'll feel for the first time that you are really in Asia. The city is the capital of the Buryatia Republic, and the Buddhist temples around the city show that the Asian religion, Buddhism, is important to many people in this region.

Lenin's head

The first thing you see in Ulan-Ude's main square is a reminder that Buryatia is a part of the Russian Federation. A huge 7.7-m-high head of Vladimir Lenin dominates the square. Buryatia gets its name from the Buryat people who are related to the Mongols (of Mongolia), and who speak a Turkic language. Originally, they were nomads, who lived in *gers* (yurts), and moved from place to place with their animals. Take a trip to the Ethnographic Museum to see some of these traditional shelters for yourself.

Russian Buddhism

Another trip takes you to the Buddhist monastery at Ivolginsky Datsan. The Soviet communist government disapproved of all religions, and from the 1930s, shut down and destroyed Buddhist temples in the USSR. This situation began to change after the Second World War, and in 1946 Stalin gave permission for a new Buddhist monastery to be built in Buryatia. Today, Ivolginsky Datsan is the impressive centre of Russian Buddhism.

▼ A statue of Buddha sits in the centre of the Ivolginsky Datsan Monastery.

Siberian tiger

The forests of the Sikhote-Alin Mountains, northeast of Vladivostok, are home to the Siberian tiger, also known as the Amur tiger. It hunts other large animals, such as bears, deer and wild boars. The Siberian tiger was hunted almost to extinction in the 1940s, and today it is still on the endangered list. It is estimated there are only around 500 Siberian tigers living in the wild.

▶ This magnificent animal is the largest of all the tiger species – it can grow up to 3 m long.

Explore Vladivostok

At the end of the line is Vladivostok, Russia's largest Pacific port, home to the Russian Navy's Pacific fleet. Founded in 1860, the city sits at the end of a hilly peninsula overlooking Golden Horn Bay. For a great view, take the city's funicular railway up to a lookout point across the bay. Then you can hop onto a tram to visit the Second World War S-56 submarine on the waterfront.

▼ Golden Horn Bay takes its name from a Turkish waterway.

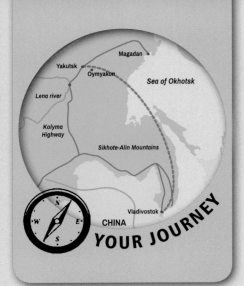

VLADIVOSTOK TO YAKUTSK

From Vladivostok, you take a flight northwest to Yakutsk in the Sakha Republic – the coldest city in the world. The region around Yakutsk is an important centre for diamond and gold mining and, despite the extreme climate, the city is home to around 280,000 people. During the winter, the average temperature is around -40°C and the city is often covered in a thick freezing fog. Summers can be hot with temperatures up to 35°C.

Road of Bones

Despite the freezing temperatures, travelling by road in the region is easier in the winter on the ice and snow than in the summer. As temperatures rise, the ground becomes soft and muddy, and the warmth brings out vast swarms of midges and mosquitoes. The Kolyma Highway, linking Yakutsk to Magadan 2,200 km to the west on the Pacific coast, is only usable during the winter. It was built by prisoners from the region's gulags (see page 18). Thousands died in the cold, and many of their bodies are buried in the road itself.

▶ The notorious Kolyma Highway is also known as the 'Road of Bones'.

The permafrost makes ice skating a favourite activity in Yakutsk.

▲ A Sakha man tends his cooking pot.

Permafrost

Yakutsk is a city built on stilts. It sits on ground that is frozen all year round, called permafrost. But when the top layer of the soil melts slightly, the ground becomes very unstable. All of the buildings in the city must be supported by stilts, driven deep into the ground, to prevent them collapsing. Take a visit to Permafrost Kingdom – set in tunnels inside a frozen hill just outside the city. You'll marvel at the ice sculptures and can even take a ride on an ice slide.

Summer and winter trips

In the summer months, when the rivers are free from ice, you can take a cruise to see the Lena Pillars. These spectacular limestone rock pillars along the Lena river were formed by the effects of the extreme climate in the region. In the winter, you could drive the 650 km northeast to Oymyakon, and take a reindeer-sledding tour out into the mountains. You'll need to take your warmest clothes, though – Oymyakon holds the record for being the coldest inhabited place on Earth.

The Sakha

The Sakha (sometimes called Yakut) are the local people of the region. In the south, their traditional occupations are farming for food, fur, leather and transport; while in the colder north, they are reindeer-herders and hunters. The small Yakut horses are incredibly hardy – they can survive without shelter in temperatures as low as -70°C. The Sakha diet is based around dairy products made from cow or mare's (female horse) milk. They also eat raw frozen fish, reindeer and horsemeat. If you get the chance, try out some of these delicacies at *Ysyakh* – the Sakha New Year festival held annually all over the region in June.

► The Lena Pillars reach up to 100 m high.

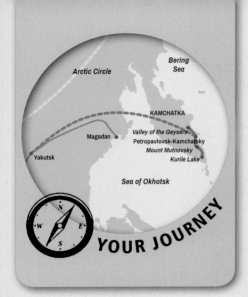

Arctic Circle

Bering
Sea

KAMCHATKA

Magadan

Valley of the Geysers
Petropavlovsk-Kamchatsky
Mount Mutnovsky
Kurile Lake

Yakutsk

Sea of Okhotsk

N
W · E
S

YOUR JOURNEY

YAKUTSK TO PETROPAVLOVSK-KAMCHATSKY

The last leg of your journey takes you to the wild and remote Kamchatka Peninsula at the eastern extremity of Russia. You can fly from Yakutsk to the city of Petropavlovsk-Kamchatsky, on the Pacific coast, but once you're there, many of the main attractions are reachable only by helicopter. It is worth it though to see the spectacular volcanoes, lakes and geysers that cover the peninsula.

Helicopter rides

Your first helicopter ride takes you about 180 km northeast of Petropavlovsk to the Valley of the Geysers on the eastern coast of the peninsula. Water from an active volcano flows through this valley, resulting in many hot springs and geysers – places where hot water and steam are forced high into the air through a hole in the Earth's crust. It is an incredible sight. Another helicopter ride delivers you to Kurile Lake, a vast and beautiful crater-lake in the south of the peninsula. You may catch a glimpse of the bears that visit the lake in the summer to catch salmon. Make sure that you go with a guide, though – the bears can be extremely dangerous to humans, so it is best to watch from a safe distance!

▼ The Kamchatka Peninsula has the largest population of brown bears in the world. These are bear cubs.

Giant crab

Back in Petropavlovsk, try some local delicacies before heading off on your next trip. Kamchatka is famed for its fish, particularly salmon, and for the Kamchatka crab. This giant crab can have a leg span of up to 1.8 m, and lives in the cold depths of the Bering Sea.

▲ A diver surfaces with two Kamchatka crabs.

Volcano walk

After your crab feast, you are ready for your final challenge – a hike into an active volcano. Mount Mutnovsky can be driven to as it lies only 60 km south of Petropavlovsk. You can go into the volcano's crater through fields of fumaroles – openings in the Earth's crust that send out scalding hot steam and gases, such as sulphur. You will need a guide – it is not a safe place to go alone. The weather can change very quickly and this is an active volcano that erupted as recently as 1960.

▶ Steaming fumaroles can be quite smelly because of the gases coming out of them.

The Kurils

If you'd like to start planning your next jouney, go to the south of Kamchatka to the long string of islands that spread like stepping stones south to Japan. They are called the Kuril Islands. Russia controls these islands, although Japan lays claim to some of the islands at the southern end of the chain. The islands are part of the 'Ring of Fire' – an area around the Pacific Ocean at the edges of tectonic plates where there are frequent earthquakes and volcanic eruptions. The islands are in fact the tops of huge undersea volcanoes. Earthquakes in this area can set off giant waves, called tsunamis.

GLOSSARY

ailments
Illnesses, usually not very serious ones.

Arctic Circle
An imaginary line around the Earth, called a line of latitude. North of this line is the Arctic region.

assassinate
Murder an important person for political or religious reasons.

Buddhism
The religion based on the teachings of Buddha, believed to have lived c.563–483 BCE or c.480–400 BCE.

Caucasus
The region at the border of Europe and Asia, between the Black Sea and the Caspian Sea.

commercial
Related to the buying or selling of goods.

communist
A social and economic system in which all property and resources are owned by the state, and wealth is divided according to individual need.

continental climate
A usually dry climate with very hot summers and very cold winters.

cosmonaut
The Russian term for an astronaut.

Cyrillic alphabet
A writing system developed by Slavic-speaking people in the 800s. The Russian alphabet is based on Cyrillic script.

delta
The area where a river divides into several smaller streams before flowing into the sea.

dictator
A ruler who has complete power and has usually obtained it by force.

dormant volcano
A volcano that has not erupted for the past 10,000 years but which could erupt again.

ecosystem
All the living things that share an environment.

embalmed
Describes something that is dead and has been treated with chemicals to preserve it.

endangered
When an animal or plant is in danger of becoming extinct (dying out forever).

freight
Goods that are transported by air, or on land or sea.

funicular railway
A railway that takes carriages up and down a steep slope.

glacier
A large slow-moving mass of ice formed in cold regions from compacted snow.

gorge
A narrow, deep valley.

gulag
The system of forced labour camps in the USSR where many prisoners died.

hydroelectric power
Electricity that is produced by the power of running water.

hydrofoil
A very fast boat that rises partly out of the water when moving at high speeds.

icon
A religious picture of Jesus Christ, or one of the saints, used in the Orthodox Church.

invertebrate
An animal without a backbone such as an insect or worm.

irrigation
The process of watering fields to grow crops.

karst
Landscape formed where rocks, such as limestone, are dissolved by water.

kremlin
A Russian fortress.

mare
An adult female horse.

mausoleum
A building in which the bodies of dead people are buried.

medieval
Relating to the Middle Ages.

mineral
A natural substance found in the Earth that is pure, or the same all the way through, and not a mixture.

monastery
A building that is home to a community of monks.

mosaic
A picture or pattern made from an arrangement of small pieces of coloured glass, tile or stone.

nomad
A person who does not have a permanent home, but travels from place to place.

nuclear
Using energy that is created when atoms are split apart or joined together.

Orthodox Christianity
The branch of Christianity followed by many people in Russia and other eastern European countries.

patron saint
A saint who is believed to protect a particular place or person.

peasant
A poor farmer.

peninsula
A piece of land that sticks out from the mainland and is almost surrounded by water.

permafrost
Ground where the layer just below the surface is permanently frozen.

pilgrim
Someone who travels to a holy place.

prisoner of war
A person who is captured and put into prison by the enemy during a war.

settled
Living in a village or town, rather than moving from place to place.

Slavic
Describes a group of languages that includes Russian, Polish, Czech and Bulgarian.

steppe
A large area of flat grassland with very few trees in Siberia and eastern Europe.

tectonic plate
One of the massive sections that form the Earth's surface, which are constantly moving.

time zone
One of the 24 divisions in the world that keep the same time.

tundra
The vast treeless region of the Arctic where the ground is permanently frozen.

venerate
To treat with great respect.

zero gravity
The state of weightlessness experienced in space.

BOOKS TO READ

Lonely Planet Russia (Travel Guide) by Simon Richmond (Lonely Planet, 2015)

DK Eyewitness Travel Guide Russia (Dorling Kindersley, 2016)

Insight Guides: Russia (APA Publications, 2016)

The Land and People: Russia (Wayland, 2016)

Developing World: Russia and Moscow (Franklin Watts, 2016)

WEBSITES

The Rough Guide website is a fantastic resource for planning a journey round Russia, telling you where to go, when to go and all the essentials you will need to know.
www.roughguides.com/destinations/europe/russia/

Lonely Planet's website invites you to visit onion-domed fairy-tale cities, cosy gingerbread wooden houses, and Russia's amazing outdoors. There's lots of information about travel, food, drink, as well as all the practical details you'll need to know.
https://www.lonelyplanet.com/russia

You can find information about the major tourist attractions in Russia on this website, along with clear maps and many pictures.
http://travelguide.michelin.com/europe/russia

It's always a good idea to check out the official government advice before travelling in Russia. There are some areas in Russia that the Foreign Office advises against visiting.
www.gov.uk/foreign-travel-advice/russia

Note to parents and teachers:
Every effort has been made by the Publishers to ensure that the websites in this book are suitable for children, that they are of the highest educational value, and that they contain no inappropriate or offensive material. However, because of the nature of the Internet, it is impossible to guarantee that the contents of these sites will not be altered. We strongly advise that Internet access is supervised by a responsible adult.

INDEX